Oceans of the World

Pacific Ocean

Louise and Richard Spilsbury

raintree

a Capstone company — publishers for children

Raintree is an imprint of Capstone Global Library Limited, a company incorporated in England and Wales having its registered office at 7 Pilgrim Street, London, EC4V 6LB – Registered company number: 6695582

www.raintree.co.uk
myorders@raintree.co.uk

Text © Capstone Global Library Limited 2015
The moral rights of the proprietor have been asserted.

Edited by Penny West
Designed by Steve Mead
Original illustrations © Capstone Global Library Ltd 2015
Picture research by Tracy Cummins
Production by Victoria Fitzgerald
Originated by Capstone Global Library Ltd
Printed and bound in China by Leo Paper Group

ISBN 978 1 406 28751 6
18 17 16 15 14
10 9 8 7 6 5 4 3 2 1

British Library Cataloguing in Publication Data
A full catalogue record for this book is available from the British Library.

Spilsbury, Louise and Richard
Pacific Ocean. – (Oceans of the World)

Acknowledgements

We would like to thank the following for permission to reproduce photographs: Getty Images: AFP PHOTO/Robyn Beck, 19, David Wall Photo, 15 Top, Mauricio Handler, 25, Nick Hall, 18, SADATSUGU TOMIZAWA/AFP, 11; Newscom: Jonathan Alcorn/ZUMAPRESS.com, 27 Top; Shutterstock: Anton Balazh, 7, Carolina K. Smith MD, 4, cdrin, 20 Bottom, chungking, 21 Bottom, Dhoxax, 16 Bottom, DmitrySerbin, 14, EpicStockMedia, Cover Top, Fiona Ayerst, 17, Igor Plotnikov, 23, leoks, 12, leonello calvetti, Cover Middle, Naaman Abreu, 22, Tanya Puntti, Cover Bottom, Vlad61, 26 Bottom, Vladislav Gurfinkel, 13, worldswildlifewonders, 24, Zmiter, Design Element.

We would like to thank Michael Bright for his invaluable help in the preparation of this book.

Every effort has been made to contact copyright holders of material reproduced in this book. Any omissions will be rectified in subsequent printings if notice is given to the publisher.

All the Internet addresses (URLs) given in this book were valid at the time of going to press. However, due to the dynamic nature of the Internet, some addresses may have changed, or sites may have changed or ceased to exist since publication. While the author and publisher regret any inconvenience this may cause readers, no responsibility for any such changes can be accepted by either the author or the publisher.

Contents

Some words are shown in bold, **like this**. You can find out what they mean by looking in the glossary.

About the Pacific Ocean

The Pacific is one of the world's five oceans. An ocean is a huge area of salty water. The Pacific is the biggest ocean on Earth. It covers about a third of the surface of our planet.

The Pacific Ocean covers more of the surface of the Earth than all the dry land put together!

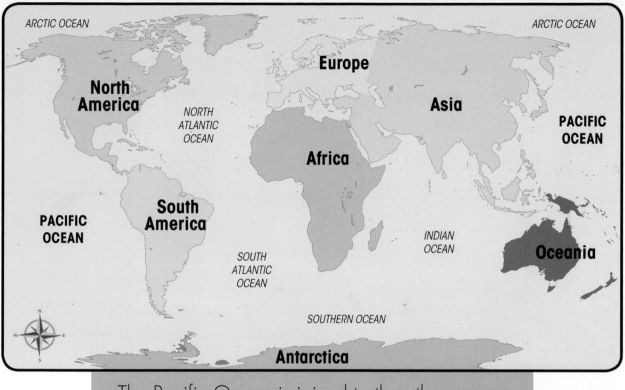

Europe

North America

NORTH ATLANTIC OCEAN

Asia

PACIFIC OCEAN

Africa

PACIFIC OCEAN

South America

SOUTH ATLANTIC OCEAN

INDIAN OCEAN

Oceania

SOUTHERN OCEAN

Antarctica

The Pacific Ocean is joined to the other oceans of the world and water flows between them.

The Pacific Ocean stretches from the Arctic Ocean in the north to the Southern Ocean in the south. To the east of the Pacific Ocean lie the **continents** of North America and South America. To the west lie the continents of Asia and Oceania.

An ocean is mostly open water. **Seas** are smaller areas of an ocean found near the land. A sea is also usually partly surrounded by land. The South China Sea, Philippine Sea, Sulu Sea and Celebes Sea are all part of the Pacific Ocean.

Several seas in the Pacific Ocean lie off the east coast of Asia.

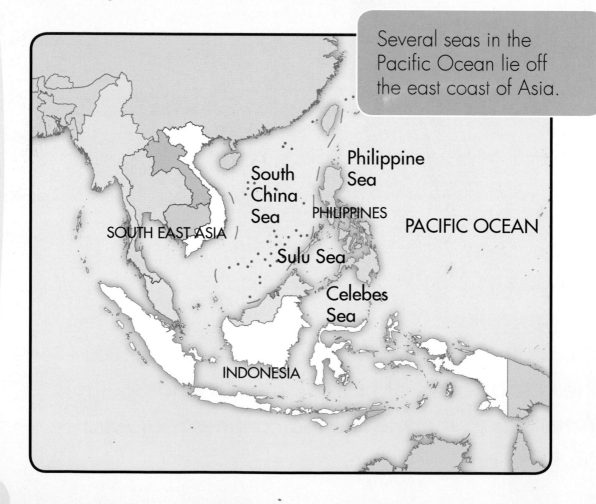

South China Sea

Philippine Sea

PHILIPPINES

PACIFIC OCEAN

SOUTH EAST ASIA

Sulu Sea

Celebes Sea

INDONESIA

Arctic Ocean

Ships travel through the Bering Strait from the Pacific Ocean to the Arctic Ocean.

Bering Strait

Bering Sea

Pacific Ocean

The Bering Sea is a sea at the far north of the Pacific Ocean. At the top of this sea is the Bering Strait. A **strait** is a narrow corridor of water that links a sea to an ocean.

Geography

The bottom of the ocean has different features, just like the land we live on. In the centre of the Pacific, the ocean floor is fairly flat. In some places there are underwater mountains with steep sides and flat tops. These are called seamounts.

Pacific Ocean fact file	
Surface area (excluding adjacent seas):	165,250,000 square kilometres (63,800,000 square miles)
Average depth:	About 4,000 metres (13,123 feet)
Deepest point:	The Mariana Trench 10,924 metres (35,840 feet) below sea level
Size of the Mariana Trench:	2,540 kilometres (1,580 miles) long and 69 kilometres (43 miles) at the widest point

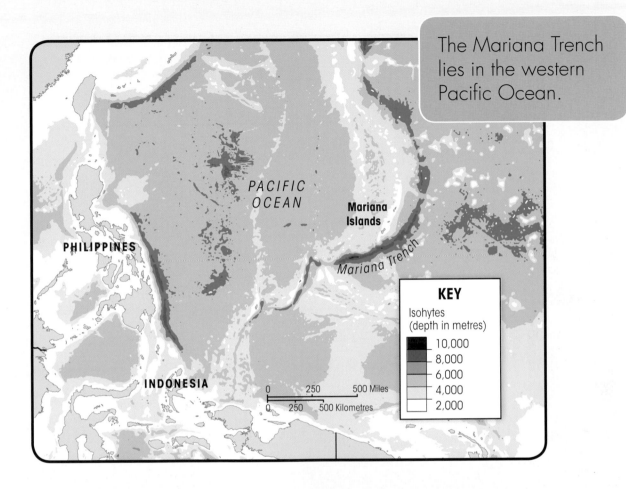

PACIFIC OCEAN

Mariana Islands

Mariana Trench

PHILIPPINES

INDONESIA

0   250   500 Miles

0   250   500 Kilometres

KEY

Isohytes
(depth in metres)

10,000
8,000
6,000
4,000
2,000

There are also deep trenches in the Pacific. A trench is a very long, deep, narrow ditch. The biggest Pacific trench is the Mariana Trench. The Challenger Deep in the Marianna Trench is the deepest point on Earth!

The edge of the Pacific Ocean is known as the Ring of Fire because most **volcanoes** are created here. The Earth's surface is split into pieces called **plates**. Beneath the Pacific Ocean is the Pacific plate. Volcanoes happen when hot liquid rock from inside the Earth rises up in the gap where plates meet.

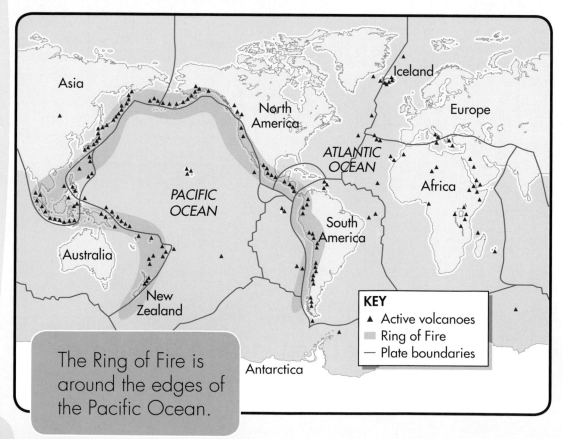

The Ring of Fire is around the edges of the Pacific Ocean.

KEY
▲ Active volcanoes
▬ Ring of Fire
— Plate boundaries

Giant tsunami waves can crash onto land and cause terrible damage and destruction.

Most of the world's **earthquakes** happen in the Ring of Fire, too. When the Pacific plate scrapes against another plate, the ground shakes and causes an earthquake. When there is an earthquake under the **sea**, this can cause a giant wave called a tsunami.

Temperature

The Pacific Ocean is so big that its water has different temperatures. Near the **Poles** it is very cold so the water is freezing and can turn to ice. Near the **Equator** the water in the Pacific Ocean is warmer.

Many tourists visit beaches around the Equator where the waters of the Pacific Ocean are very warm.

This is a satellite picture of a huge hurricane over the Pacific Ocean.

Typhoons or hurricanes sometimes form over the Pacific Ocean. These are huge whirling winds that happen when warm ocean water heats the air above it. The warm air rises and this causes winds. When hot air rises quickly, the winds spin very quickly, too.

Islands

There are 25,000 islands in the Pacific, which is more than in any other ocean! An island is an area of land surrounded by water. New Zealand is a country made up of two large islands and many smaller islands in the south-western Pacific Ocean.

This lovely beach is on North Island, one of New Zealand's two main islands.

The Fijian archipelago is in the South Pacific Ocean.

The country of Fiji is made up of an **archipelago** of different islands. An archipelago is a group or row of islands close together. There are more than 800 islands in Fiji including over 500 small islands called islets.

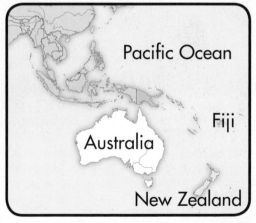

Pacific Ocean

Fiji

Australia

New Zealand

Some Pacific islands are old **volcanoes**. When a volcano **erupts** underwater, the hot, liquid rock cools down quickly and becomes solid rock. The top of this volcanic rock can poke above the water to form an island!

Hawaii

Pacific Ocean

Australia

New Zealand

This island in Hawaii formed from a volcano.

This colourful coral reef is off the coast of the Raja Ampat islands in Indonesia.

Some volcanic islands in the Pacific Ocean are surrounded by **coral reefs**. Coral is made by millions of tiny animals called polyps. Each polyp builds a skeleton of **limestone** around itself. A coral reef is made of millions of these limestone cases.

Resources

There are lots of useful resources in the
Pacific Ocean. People catch more fish here
than in any other ocean. In the cold waters
of the North Pacific Ocean, big boats
called trawlers catch fish such as salmon,
tuna and herring.

Many trawlers have
freezers on board to
store the caught fish.

People drill for oil under the ocean floor from platforms like these.

People drill under the floor of the Pacific Ocean to get oil and gas. We use these fuels for energy to power vehicles and other machines. People take sand and gravel from the ocean floor for building. They also dig up copper and other metals to make things such as mobile phones.

Ports

Lots of ships carry goods and people across the Pacific Ocean. Seattle is a city with a big **port** on the west coast of North America. A port is a place where ships load and unload.

Seattle

North America

People can get on a cruise ship in Seattle and travel to Alaska and Canada.

Ships take things made in China across the Pacific to sell all over the world.

Asia

Shanghai

PACIFIC OCEAN

The port at Shanghai is very busy. Shanghai is a city on the east coast of China. Cranes load containers full of computers, toys and other goods onto ships.

People

Many people work on the coasts around the Pacific Ocean. In Mexico there are huge hotels where tourists come to visit the beaches. Many people work here in the hotels, restaurants and shops.

Some workers take tourists out on boats or on other trips.

Fishing families live in these stilt houses on beaches in the Philippines.

Some people in Washington state, USA live in houseboats on the Pacific Ocean. In the Philippines, some families live in houses on wooden legs called stilts. This keeps the houses dry when the **tide** comes in.

Animals

There are many different animals in the Pacific Ocean. Sea otters live near the coast. They dive to catch clams, crabs and other small animals underwater. They eat lying on their backs on the water's surface.

Sea otters wrap themselves in seaweed so they don't float away while they snooze!

The giant Pacific octopus can be as big as 9 metres (30 feet) across, when spread out across the ground!

The giant Pacific octopus is the biggest octopus in the world. These amazing animals catch fish, shrimp and other animals with their long arms. They can change colour to hide against rocks on the floor of the Pacific Ocean.

Famous places

One of the most famous places in the Pacific Ocean is the Great Barrier Reef. This is the biggest **coral reef** in the world. It runs more than 2,000 kilometres (1,250 miles) along the north-east coast of Australia. It contains many beautiful, different coloured corals.

Great Barrier Reef

Australia

Sea turtles, dolphins and many other amazing animals live on the Great Barrier Reef.

This plastic waste from the Great Pacific Garbage Patch washed up on a beach in Hawaii.

United States

Great Pacific Garbage Patch

Mexico

The Great Pacific Garbage Patch is not beautiful. It is an enormous area of plastic waste floating in the Pacific Ocean. It has been called the biggest rubbish dump in the world. Some of the waste is too small to see, but all of it is bad for the ocean and the animals in it.

Fun facts

- The Great Barrier Reef is the only living thing on Earth that astronauts can see from space.

- Over 65 per cent of the world's fish caught from the oceans comes from the Pacific Ocean.

- The word 'pacific' means peaceful. The explorer Magellan gave the Pacific Ocean its name because the waters were calm when he first discovered it in 1521.

- If Mount Everest was put into the deepest part of the Mariana Trench then its top would still be 2 kilometres (1.4 miles) underwater.

- The centre of the Pacific Ocean is 2,688 kilometres (1,670 miles) from the nearest land, making it the most remote point on Earth!

Quiz

1 Which is the biggest ocean on Earth?

2 Which is the deepest **trench** on Earth?

3 Why is the area round the Pacific Ocean called the Ring of Fire?

4 Where is the world's biggest rubbish dump?

Glossary

archipelago group or row of islands close together

continent one of seven huge areas of land on Earth

coral reef long line of stony coral rock near the surface of the ocean

earthquake sudden and violent shaking of the ground

erupt when a volcano explodes and hot, melted rock called lava and dust spurts out of it

Equator imaginary line around the middle of the Earth

limestone type of hard rock or stone

plate giant piece of rock that floats on the hot rock in the centre of the Earth

Poles the two points at opposite ends of the Earth, the North Pole and South Pole

port place at the edge of an ocean where ships stop

sea smaller area of an ocean usually found near the land and usually partly surrounded by land

strait narrow corridor of water that links seas and oceans

tide the way the sea moves up and down the shore twice a day

volcano hole in the Earth from which fiery hot, melted rock called lava spurts out

Find out more

Books
Deep Oceans (Earth's Last Frontiers), Ellen Labrecque (Raintree, 2014)

Ocean (Eyewitness), Miranda MacQuitty (Dorling Kindersley, 2014)

Amazing Habitats: Oceans, Leon Gray (Franklin Watts, 2014)

Websites
Videos, images and facts about the deep ocean can be found at
www.bbc.co.uk/nature/habitats/Deep_sea

Learn about threats to oceans and coasts at
wwf.panda.org/about_our_earth/blue_planet/problems

Find out how the Pacific Ocean got its name at
http://oceanservice.noaa.gov/facts/pacific.html

Index